Table of Content

Chapter 1..........2

chapter2.........3

chapter3............4

Chapter4............11

Chapter5.............13

Chapter6..............35

Chapter7...............62

Chapter 1

BODY ART TATTOO

A tattoo is a form of body modification made by inserting tattoo ink, dyes, and/or pigments, either indelible or temporary, into the dermis layer of the skin to form a design. Tattoo artists create these designs using several tattooing processes and techniques, including hand-tapped traditional tattoos and modern tattoo machines. The history of tattooing goes back to Neolithic times, practiced across the globe by many cultures, and the symbolism and impact of tattoos vary in different places and cultures.

An example of a tattoo design

Application of a tattoo to a woman's foot
Tattoos may be decorative (with no specific meaning), symbolic (with a specific meaning to the wearer), or pictorial (a depiction of a specific person or item). Many tattoos serve as rites of passage, marks of status and rank, symbols of religious and spiritual devotion, decorations for bravery, marks of fertility, pledges of love, amulets and talismans, protection, and punishment, like the marks of outcasts, slaves, and convicts. Extensive decorative tattooing has also been part of the work of performance artists such as tattooed ladies.

Today, people choose to be tattooed for artistic, cosmetic, sentimental/memorial, religious, and spiritual reasons, and to symbolize their belonging to or identification with particular groups, including criminal gangs (see criminal tattoos) or a particular ethnic group or law-abiding subculture. Tattoos may show how a person feels about a relative (commonly a parent or child) or an unrelated person.

Tattoos can also be used for functional purposes, such as identification, permanent makeup, and medical purposes

chapter 2

HOW TO GET A TATTOO

1. CHOOSE THE RIGHT TATTOO ARTIST
Once you've decided to go under the gun, the next step is to choose a tattoo artist that's right for you. Your inking will be around as long as you are, so first off, take your time. Talk to like-minded friends, visit studios, scrutinize different portfolios, and talk to the artists.

2. SELECTING THE RIGHT TATTOO FOR YOU
Just like buying a pair of shoes, when it comes to choosing the right tattoo, it's not a one-size-fits-all. If you're going to be comfortable with your ink for years to come, there are several factors to consider. Think carefully about the style, size, and type of design you want. Next, make a list of your favorite things and gather inspiration from Instagram and online publications. Finally, chat with your tattoo artist about the different tattoo ideas for men.

3. TRUST THE PROFESSIONALS
Trust in your tattoo professional is key when it comes to getting inked. It's essential to have a good rapport and understanding with the person marking you for life. First, if the state requires one, find a reputable tattoo artist with a license. Look out for any diplomas, awards, or professional training paperwork on the studio walls. Once you've established you're in safe hands, you can sit back and relax.

4. TAKING CARE OF YOUR TATTOO
Aftercare is an important step in getting inked. Its effects are much more than skin deep, and this is why you must keep your new tat healthy with a tattoo lotion. Follow your tattoo artist's instructions to the letter, and your artwork will rock for many years to come.

chapter 3

Health

23 Things You Need to Know Before Getting Your First Tattoo

Getting your first tattoo is both terrifying and exciting, and you probably have a million questions already. How bad will it hurt? How do you know if a parlor is safe? How much will it cost? Before you get anything permanently placed on your body, you should make sure every single one of your pressing questions is answered.

1. Prices vary depending on size.

Tattoo parlors adjust prices based on the size and style of the tattoo you want. And FYI, if they know you're a virgin, they might try to up the price on you. It's a good idea to call and ask for an estimate before you go in, although that number may change slightly once the design is drawn. If you can, bring someone who has gotten inked before to help you negotiate or do research on pricing beforehand to make sure you don't get ripped off.

2. DON'T go bargain hunting.

Many parlors have minimum prices (usually $50 or $100), so a tiny heart tattoo, for example, shouldn't cost much more than that. If someone is willing to do your tattoo for $15...something's off. Sketchy artists could mean infections and shoddy work. Since your tattoo will be on your body for life and your health could be at risk, it's an investment worth the money.

That being said, some parlors do legit tattoo sales for holidays,). They're called "flash sales" and you pick a pre-drawn design for a discounted price.

Other than that, though, tattoo shopping isn't the time to bargain shop. Instead, save up for a professional, reputable tattoo artist. "If you can't afford to be tattooed by the artist that you want, you need to wait until you can instead of settling for 'fast food,'"

3. You can be allergic to tattoo ink.

"True allergic reactions to tattoos, and the ink, are very, very possible, but thankfully not super common. Often people with sensitive skin mount a reaction to the prep process that cleans and sterilizes the skin, which is more common than a true allergic reaction to the ink and tattoo itself."

If you do react badly, the tattoo might break out in an itchy red rash like mine.

4. You have to be 18 to get one.

Yep, like voting and scary movies, you've gotta be 18 to get inked. Some states will allow you to get a tattoo earlier with a parent's permission while you're still underaged, though.

5. Look into the parlor beforehand.

Just because the tattoo parlor is within walking distance from your dorm, doesn't mean it's a quality shop (I learned this one the hard way, btw). Visit the parlor, ask about their artists' licenses, and also check out reviews online – Yelp will give you all that tea. Tattooing laws differ by state, so you should research the guidelines in your state and make sure anywhere you're considering has the proper licensing and adheres to those guidelines.

"It's very important for a client to feel comfortable with how clean the studio is," "Ask an artist: What do you do to clean in between tattoos? How often do you clean this station I'm going to be tattooed on? What kind of surface do you tattoo off of?'"

6. The parlor should be spotless (like, spotless).

Getting a tattoo isn't a minor change, like coloring your hair. Another human being is *literally* creating an open wound that can get infected if the shop isn't taking proper precautions. Though it's much more important how the surfaces and tools are being sanitized, the shop should look and smell as clean as a hospital.

7. Make sure the artist uses a new, disposable needle and ink cup, and wears clean gloves.

Reusing needles can spread infection or cause you to contract a serious illness, like HIV or Hepatitis B. Yeah, this sh*It is serious. So your artist should use a brand new, single-use needle and use all new cups, napkins, and gloves. Watch to make sure they open the needle package in front of you to ensure it's clean.

This content is imported from a poll. You may be able to find the same content in another format, or you may be able to find more information on their website.

8. Check that the surface you're getting tattooed on is a non-porous material.

Porous materials, like wood or marble, can be difficult to fully sanitize, so it's not a good option for a tattoo station. "A porous surface, like rock and marble, would not be something that your tattoo station should be made of," says McCurdy. "It should be stainless steel or a sterilizable material like stainless."

9. The way the design looks in the sketch is how it will look on your skin.

The artist will outline your tattoo before they apply it, so make sure you're especially observant when you correct the design. The drawing you approve will go directly onto your body and the artist will use it as tracing for the final tattoo. Be extra aware of spelling (it's not common that you'll get a misspelled tattoo, but it does happen), and don't be afraid to speak up about any changes you want. Remember: this is forever.

10. If the artist makes you feel uncomfortable, leave.

If they get sassy when you ask them to adjust the design, leave. If they shame your tattoo idea, leave. If they just generally make you feel weird or uncomfortable, leave. Getting your first tattoo is scary and they shouldn't be adding to your nerves or making you feel bad.

"I think that in our industry it's a common thing where a young girl is going to come in to speak to an artist and is going to be met with a nose-in-the-air kind of attitude, like 'I don't want to do this girl's silly tattoo,'" "I don't think that it's a fair thing or that a client should put up with that. You should find someone who wants to get your tattoo."

11. Bigger tattoos can take more than one session to complete.

Larger designs or ones with a lot of colors can take multiple sessions to finish, so your tattoo might not be complete after your first visit. A bigger design with a lot of detail or color might take two sessions, while an entire sleeve could take months (and hundreds to thousands of dollars) to finish. On the other hand, a simple tattoo, like a small black star, should only take about 5 minutes. If you want a better idea of the timeline, ask your artist to give you an estimate of how long it will take before you get started.

12. Think about your tattoo for at least a year before you commit to it.

"When [you're] designing, try to think of the word 'timeless' because your tattoo will be timeless, even if your design is not," What you think will look cool may change so you want to think hard about the design and make sure you will still be into it months later. Remember: your tastes may change over time but this will last forever.

Getting inked might seem like a fun thing to do with your friends on spring break or before graduation, getting a spur-of-the-moment is probably not a great idea. "Think twice before jumping into a tattoo," "Don't do it on a whim, don't do it when you're drinking — those are all the stories I get from my patients. Tattoos of boyfriends and girlfriends [are] a no-no — people always regret it."

13. Don't get inked before your beach vacation.

The quote you want on your rib cage will look great with that cut-out swimsuit, but tattoos take at least two weeks to heal, so you won't be able to swim (pool chemicals and ocean bacteria are bad for a healing tattoo) or hang out in direct sunlight (even healed tattoos are sensitive to UV rays) if you get it on or right before spring break. Your best bet: Just wait until you get home and make sure to stay out of the sun, ocean, or pool for at least two weeks after you get inked.

14. You'll probably have to get your tattoo touched up.

Tattoos fade over time, no matter how well you treat them because your skin is always shedding new layers. So you'll probably have to go back under the needle at some point to keep it in tip-top shape. You can go to any artist to get it touched up, but if you liked your original artist, it's always best to go back to them. A lot of parlors will give you a touch-up for free, but others charge. Like normal tattoos, touch-up pricing varies based on the amount of work you need to do, so if you're curious, ask your artist for an estimate or check the parlor's website – they'll likely have a touch-up policy outlined under their FAQs.

15. Tattoos fade faster when exposed to sunlight.

"There are certain parts of your skin that are exposed to more sun, so pigments can break down quicker," "Like the outside of your arm, it will age differently than the inside of your arm that isn't exposed to as much sun throughout your life." If you're outside a lot and worried about fading, consider getting inked in a spot that's less exposed like the inside of your wrist, and always, always, always wear sunscreen, especially on your ink.

16. The pain depends on the tattoo placement.

Disclaimer: getting a tattoo will not hurt. Pain tolerance differs for each person, but generally, tattoos placed right over bones tend to hurt the most. A tattoo on your foot or ribs might be an 8 on a scale of 1 to 10, while a bicep only is a 4. And of course, the bigger the tattoo, the longer you'll be in pain. Speaking from personal experience, my foot, ribcage, and spine hurt the worst (in that order), while tattoos on my hands and arms were much more tolerable.

17. If you don't end up liking your tattoo, you can get it covered up.

It's pretty easy to get a tattoo covered up, especially if it's small. A good artist can put a new design over it, covering the original tattoo completely — some parlors even specialize in cover-ups. So even if you do change your mind one day, you won't be stuck with a tattoo that you hate.

18. You can also get tattoos removed.

You can get your tattoo removed with a laser treatment. Depending on the ink color, stubbornness of the ink, and size of the tattoo, it can take up to several sessions. Blue, black, and green inks are easier to remove with laser treatment because the lasers can detect those colors more easily and thus, remove them more accurately, Lighter colors, like yellow and white, on the other hand, are more difficult to remove. But keep in mind that while the process eliminates the tattoo, it can leave scarring and the procedure can be pricey.

1 9. Tattoo removal doesn't hurt if you go to a doctor.

Salons offer the service, but since they are not medical professionals, you should never go to one for tattoo removal. Go to a real, licensed doctor to get the procedure done – it's safer and pain-free, because like in a salon doctors can numb the area beforehand.

"Removing [a tattoo is not painful at all. If you go to a doctor, the doctor will numb it... with a local anesthetic," "When you read about people who say tattoo removal is painful, it's because they're not going to doctors. They're going to various spas, not medical doctors. Spas cannot administer anesthetic injections. A doctor can administer local anesthetics, so you'll feel zero pain."

20. You might not be able to get the exact tattoo you want.

If you want to get a lyric in a reny font, your artist might refuse – and for good reason. If a font is too small, it can bleed together over time and turn into a smudge. Instead, the designer might ask you to compromise with a slightly bigger font. Remember: Your artist is a professional, so if they have some serious feelings about the logistics of your design, hear them out.

21. They might shave you first.

If you're getting a tattoo on your arm or another particularly hairy part of your body, the artist might shave the spot beforehand — as the doctor would before surgery (this is an open wound, after all). You can ask in advance if you should shave the area before coming in, but most tattoos don't require it.

22. It will itch afterward.

After about a week (sometimes sooner) new tattoos will start to have a mild itch – but whatever you do, DON'T scratch it. Your fingernails can peel off the ink, leaving spots of un-tattooed skin on your tattoo. (If you do accidentally scratch some ink off, though, your artist can fix it easily with a touch-up. Scratching can also lead to infection, so instead, slap your tattoo gently with a clean hand for relief. You can also use a Cortisone cream to take away the itch safely.

If the itching becomes unbearable or your tattoo breaks out in a rash (photos of that above), go to urgent care or a dermatologist ASAP.

23. Avoid long showers while you're healing.

It's important to keep your new ink clean by gently washing the area with antibacterial soap and water, then patting it dry three times a day. A little water won't hurt it, but try to avoid spending too much time in the shower (no baths, please) after getting inked. Soaking your tattoo isn't good for it, because the water will slow down the healing process by deteriorating your newly-forming skin. If you get a design on a part of your body that gets a lot of water in the shower, like your back, try to keep your showers short and limit the area's contact with water until it heals.

Chapter 4

12 classic tattoo styles you need to know

Here are twelve of the classic styles of tattoo art, the ones you want to know before you start getting into tattoo design. If you're looking for the perfect tattoo style, you may not be able to use the exact terminology of what you want, but in all likelihood, you'll have one of these in mind already. Figuring out exactly how you want your perfect tattoo to look is hard, but we hope the styles below will help you narrow it down.

1. Classic Americana tattoo

These may be the first kind of tattoo you think of, an old-school style defined by bold outlines and the use of similar colors and imagery. They're closely tied to the ocean and nautical imagery, pinup female figures, fierce predatory animals, or combinations of hearts, roses, and daggers.

2. New school tattoo style

New School tattoos are like a crazy comic book on your body. Jesse Smith's work is famous in this category, depicting fabulous imagined worlds full of chaos and very often caricatured animals in vivid color.

3. Japanese tattoo style

As we showed you in a previous post, there are centuries of history for the art of tattooing all over the world. One that has maintained its popularity is the Japanese-style Irezumi. Tattoo artists still create both traditional and new takes on these classic masterpieces. And it's a genre particularly known for large images that cover the back, arms, and legs.

Here, Chris O'Donnell of New York shows off the traditional animal, floral, and samurai imagery of this style.

4. Black and grey tattoo style

Jessica Mascitti of LA's East Side Tattoo shows us great examples of different kinds of work in a genre that can encompass a wide range of styles. Black and grey images aren't as limited by subject matter, depicting anything and everything realistically in shades of grey, originally done by watering down black ink to create a spectrum of shades.

5. Portraiture tattoo

Shane O'Neill shows us how realistic you can get with tattoos with his portraiture, a sub-set of the realism genre (which is just like it sounds—realistic renderings of imagery). Without the black outlines of some of the more classic styles, artists can achieve eerily accurate renditions of people both in color and black and grey.

6. Stick and poke tattoo

Artist Slowerblack shows off the possibilities of the stick-n-poke, where the artist uses a single needle to create simple designs. Recently popularized for DIY tattoo-ers, in the hands of a professional this art can go to beautiful levels, characterized by thick and bold lines most often in simple black with small decorative patterns.

7. Realism tattoo

Realistic tattoos can portray anything from scenery or objects to animals and people. Whether colorful or in black and white, this is a classic tattoo style that is ideal if there's something very specific you want to portray. Realistic tattoos are hard to get perfectly right and it takes a skilled tattoo artist or tattoo designer to create a realistic-looking artwork with amazing visual impact.

8. Blackwork tattoo style

Blackwork is a tattoo style originally derived from the original tribal tattoos, made of thick and bold black lines in a variety of geometric shapes. But artists continue to take this genre to new levels, incorporating patterns and imagery derived from all sorts of sources into mesmerizing pieces swirling in different forms around the body, like these from Nazareno Tubaro (who also created the featured image!)

9. Biomechanical tattoo

Typically freehanded, Biomechanical tattoos adapt to the unique flow of a person's body, meant to mimic machinery that could be hidden within the skin. It's hard to get away from Roman Abrego's name when you bring up these bad boys—his alien and mechanical-inspired images covering often the arms and legs of his clients.

10. Geometric tattoo style

Geometric tattoos are very popular right now and can be timeless when done right. They can either feature geometric elements only or have a combination of geometric and organic (often floral or natural) elements. The contrast between the exact, sharp lines of this tattoo style and the curves of the body makes them stand out boldly.

11. Realistic Trash Polka tattoo

Realistic Trash Polka was created by Germany's Buena Vista Tattoo Club. Created by Simone Plaff and Volko Merschky, it's instantly recognizable for its collage-like structure, intricate and sampling from printed materials—from photography to hand-writing, paint splashes to type-writing.

12. Surrealism tattoo style

The art genre of surrealism gives artists loads of material to work with. The artistic style can change, and the subject can change, but as long as the viewer comes out of the experience with that feeling of sublime fantasy, the artist has achieved their purpose. Pictured here are the amazing works of Milanese tattoo artist Pietro Sedda, owner of the shop Saint Mariner.

Chapter 5

121 BEST TATTOO IDEAS FOR MEN

TATTOO IDEAS FOR MEN

1. SMALL TATTOO

One of the most go-to tattoo ideas for men, small tattoo designs are incredibly versatile. They look good almost anywhere on the body, and what's more, they are easy to conceal. Your ink needn't be super-sized to make a statement, from a meaningful quote on the chest to a discreet yet detailed design on the wrist.

2. SIMPLE TATTOO

Simple tattoos use crisp lines, a sparse color palette, and negative space for a clean and smart look. Simple designs are a cool tattoo idea for men who would describe themselves as classy yet understated.

3. TIGER TATTOO

Tiger tattoos for men symbolize a fierce, courageous personality. For alpha males who pride themselves on their inner strength and power, this big cat inking may take the form of a traditional, old-school design or ancient Japanese style.

4. BIRD TATTOO

Bird tattoos adorned the bodies of ancient Egyptians as early as 2000 BC. Fast forward to the 1700s, and sailors were wearing a swallow tattoo as a way to showcase their seagoing skills. Today, bird tattoos offer even more possibilities. The phoenix, eagle, and owl are just a few examples that have unique meanings for any man with skin in the game.

5. WOLF TATTOO

The wolf is a pack animal that fiercely protects its family. In Native American culture, the wolf has a deep spiritual meaning. It represents close family ties, loyalty, and protection. Wolf tattoo designs make cool tattoos for men who are proud of their strong family values.

6. COMPASS TATTOO

Early sailors believed a compass inking would bring fortune for a successful voyage and help guide them home safely. Likewise, compass designs are a cool tattoo idea for men who have a passion for adventure and travel. Always pointing North, this inking will help keep its wearer on the right path.

7. ANGEL TATTOO

Linking heaven and Earth, the angel is a guiding figure and embodiment of hope and innocence. An angel tattoo needn't always be literal. Angel wings or a halo can honor an absent loved one. A guardian angel symbolizes protection, or combined with a darker figure, can represent an internal struggle between good and evil. Angel designs are meaningful tattoo ideas for men.

8. CROSS TATTOO

A perfect tattoo idea for religious men, cross tattoos carry a powerful meaning. The cross is often part of an intricate design featuring rosary beads, angel wings, or Celtic line work. They're perfect for larger chest, back, and sleeve pieces. For smaller inkings, the wrist and behind the ear are popular placements.

9. ARROW TATTOO

Arrow designs are highly customizable and a cool tattoo for men. They can be a single line drawing or scaled up to make a large leg or arm piece. The arrow symbol links closely to Native American culture. Here, two crossed arrows represent alliance, while a single arrow broken in half symbolizes peace.

10. SKULL TATTOO

Many people believe skull tattoos represent death. In a lot of cases, though, they carry a less morbid meaning. This inking often serves as a reminder to its owner not to fear death and enjoy each day to the fullest. Skull tattoos lend themselves to black and gray ink.

11. DRAGON TATTOO

Dragon tattoos are prominent in almost every tattooing style around the world. In Chinese culture, they represent strength, good fortune, wisdom, and the male element, Yang. The shape of these mythical creatures is versatile enough to curve and fit almost anywhere on the body, making them cool tattoos for guys.

12. LION TATTOO

The well-beloved King of the Jungle, lions, are among the most majestic creatures in the Animal Kingdom. Lion tattoos for men serve as a powerful message to the world that their wearer is fearless, courageous, and not a man to challenge!

13. QUOTE TATTOO

Some men want their ink to be fun and light-hearted. While others want designs that represent a deeper meaning. Either way, quote tattoos are a thought-provoking way to showcase your personality, whether it's a fashion quote, a Harvey Specter quote, or simply words to live by. Wear a quote alone or pair it with complementary design elements. Just make sure the inked words have a personal meaning.

14. FAMILY TATTOO

As your grandparents may tell you, blood is thicker than water. So honor your heritage by choosing artwork that represents those closest to you. One on-trend family tattoo for men is to take a special note penned by a family member and have it inked by the artist in your loved one's handwriting.

15. STAR TATTOO

It's possible to interpret star tattoos in many ways. A Northern star symbolizes travel or a journey. A constellation can show a particular zodiac sign, and a nautical star represents the compass rose sailors used to navigate the seas. When it comes to star tattoo ideas for men, the sky is the limit.

16. OWL TATTOO

Folklore depicts the owl as a creature of knowledge, wisdom, and mystery. In modern stories like Harry Potter, the owl is a bridge between the human and magical world, acting as a close companion to their masters. Combing owl tattoos with natural elements such as trees and branches for a seriously cool tattoo for men.

17. EAGLE TATTOO

The eagle is the USA's official mascot. It stands for courage, freedom, and having an eye on the end goal. So if you're a modern guy who wants to stand proud, the eagle tattoo for men will mark you for life as brave, intelligent, and powerful.

18. NAME TATTOO

Getting a name tattooed on any part of your body is meaningful. It can be that of a parent, child, or loved one, either living or lost. The most popular placement for a name tattoo for men is the forearm. Wherever you place this important piece of artwork, wear your tattoo with pride.

19. CLOCK TATTOO

Time marches on, and a clock tattoo is there to remind us that each moment is precious. They're cool tattoo ideas for men who want to mark a special moment in life, honor an achievement, or believe in the importance of seizing the day! Also a primo tattoo for any timepiece buffs or men's watch enthusiasts.

20. ROSE TATTOO

Rose tattoos have a special meaning. Go red to symbolize love and passion, or black for mourning and loss. Body art can say a thousand words, and this inking is deeply personal. Rose tattoos for men are increasingly popular as they are the perfect way to express inner feelings through art.

21. TREE TATTOO

Tree tattoos are cool tattoos for men whose roots are planted firmly in the family. They are timeless and classic tattoo designs that will stand the test of time. Let your chest or back become the canvas for this exceptional artwork, and make sure your ink tells a story.

22. GEMINI TATTOO

The constellation of the Gemini zodiac relates to the Greek and Roman myth of twin half-brothers Castor and Pollux. Upon Castor's defeat in battle, Pollux bargained with Zeus to return him to life. Zeus granted the wish providing the twins spend half their time on Earth and half amongst the stars. The Gemini symbol represents companionship and an unbreakable bond, making the Gemini tattoo a unique idea for men.

23. CLOUD TATTOO

Depending on your outlook on life, cloud tattoos can either represent a positive silver lining or an approaching storm. Light, dreamy, and whimsical, or dark, and shadowy, the style of the cloud design will determine what your tattoo says about you.

24. TAURUS TATTOO

The Taurus constellation represents the story of the Greek god Zeus and Princess Europa. The myth tells how Zeus transformed himself into a bull to win Europa's affections and carried her across the sea to Crete. The Taurus symbol is one of love and perseverance. Taurus tattoos are an ideal tattoo for men born under this star sign.

25. CHRISTIAN TATTOO

Praying hands, angels, crosses, biblical verses, and depictions of Jesus Christ are all Christian tattoos for men that honor devotion to a higher power. With so many tattoo designs to choose from, you can easily find a Christian inking for any part of the body.

26. SCORPIO TATTOO

Scorpio is the eighth zodiac sign. Its symbol looks like the letter "M" with an arrow-tipped tail. Scorpios are passionate, profound, and loyal. If you're a tough guy who is a bit of a control freak, don't leave your choice of inking to a tattoo artist. Instead, check out scorpion tattoo ideas for men well before going under the gun.

27. AMERICAN FLAG TATTOO

An American flag tattoo is a symbol of patriotism and freedom. These inkings are a popular tattoo for men serving in the Military or Emergency Services. Fly your flag tattoo where others can easily see it; on the forearm, upper arm, chest, or back to complement your military style.

28. GRIM REAPER TATTOO

This tattoo for men represents the circle of life. Grim reaper tattoos remind us that life and death are inevitable; they convey that their wearer isn't afraid to meet their maker. This design, though, is not all gloom and doom. It's also about making the most of every moment and enjoying each day as if it were the last.

29. CELTIC TATTOO

Release your inner warrior with a Celtic tattoo. From intricate crosses to detailed knots, if you want to honor your heritage, this design is the one for you. Although Celtic warriors wore blue-colored tattoos to intimidate their enemies, popular tattoos for men today are often black with gray shadows.

30. DEMON TATTOO

Demon tattoos are powerful inkings for large areas of skin or full sleeves. Not for the faint-hearted, they make cool tattoos for men who want to show the world they're ready to tackle whatever life throws at them.

31. STAR WARS TATTOO

Star Wars tattoos for men are a fun and creative way for movie lovers to share their passion for these intergalactic characters. A colorful Yoda inking, a detailed R2D2, or a villainous Darth Vader, may the force be with you!

32. 3D TATTOO

Transcend traditional ink with a 3D tattoo. If you are a man on a mission and a committed collector of skin art, this tattoo style will become your artwork of desire. Three-dimensional designs work well in bright colors with whimsical themes and are cool tattoos for men who are anything but one-dimensional!

33. BIOMECHANICAL TATTOO

Man and machine merge as biomechanical tattoos for men become the next best body art. Robotic and unique, gears, wires, and steel combine to transform the body into living machines to create a hardcore look for the millennial man.

34. MUSIC TATTOO

For many of us, music tattoos hold great meaning, reminding us of a powerful memory, providing comfort in tough times, or helping us to celebrate the best of moments. They can commemorate a favorite song, artist (like Elvis), or instrument and create meaningful tattoos for men who love making music.

35. FEATHER TATTOO

A bird's feather can represent freedom and travel, while an angel's feather may be a tribute to a missing loved one. In Celtic times, feathers held mystical powers. While for the Egyptians, they represented Gods and Goddesses. Whichever style you choose, feather designs make versatile and unique tattoo ideas for men.

36. CROWN TATTOO

This powerful headpiece represents glory, power, royalty, and immortality. Crown tattoos for men make a clear statement that their wearer makes their own rules. A crown can also be a touching tribute to the "King" or "Queen" in your life, such as the late Kobe Bryant's crown and butterfly inking dedicated to his wife, Vanessa.

37. KING AND QUEEN TATTOO

King and Queen designs are a popular option for His and Hers tattoos. Depending on your couple's style, go literal with matching crowns and text or symbolic with intricate and elaborate designs. Either way, these are romantic and cool tattoos for men who know they've found the one.

38. SAMURAI WARRIOR TATTOO

Elite Japanese warriors from noble backgrounds were charged with defending their lords from mortal enemies, the Samurai was a fierce fighting force with a strong moral code. Channel your warrior spirit with a Samurai tattoo representing nobility, courage, power, and honor.

39. ABSTRACT TATTOO

Express yourself with an abstract tattoo for men. This skin art speaks volumes about its wearer's artistic flair and individuality. Brushstrokes, shapes, and lines create an idea of an object or person. Much more than just a trendy tattoo, it's a creative art form for the non-conformist.

40. ANIMAL TATTOO

From wild animals to domestic pets, there is an age-old belief that humans and animals are connected spiritually. So regardless of whether you're honoring a pooch that has passed away, rocking some leopard print, or wearing your lion tattoo with pride, animal tattoos have lots of ideas for men.

41. BLACKWORK TATTOO

The origins of blackwork tattoos lay within the ancient form of tribal tattoos. The difference is that they're filled in with solid black and don't have the same cultural symbolism. A popular placement for this tattoo style is in a half or full-sleeve design. They're also a viable option for cover-ups.

42. DOTWORK TATTOO

Dotwork tattoos are a design classic. It's a unique technique that combines multiple small black dots to create a striking visual effect. Dotwork may bring a full image to life or provide shading for a tattoo design. More detailed inkings can take hours of hard work, so they're ideal tattoos for men who have lots of patience!

43. GEOMETRIC TATTOO

If you're a man on a mission looking to discover a stunning symmetrical tattoo, a great choice is a geometric tattoo design. Straight lines and angles represent order and structure, while shapes and curves symbolize connection and community. They make awesome tattoos for men who are comfortable in their skin.

44. JAPANESE TATTOO

Before the Second World War, Japanese tattoos were a way to depict social status and often a punishment for slaves and criminals. On the plus side, they were also a protective and spiritual charm and a symbol of devotion. Today, Japanese-style Koi fish, geishas, dragons, tigers, and Samurai designs are cool tattoos for men.

45. LINE DRAWING TATTOO

Are you a man who enjoys the simple things in life? If you are, a line tattoo is an inspirational inking. Executed in one continuous line, it's a cool tattoo for men that can be either complex or intricate. This impressive technique needs a highly skilled tattoo artist with a steady hand.

46. MEMORIAL TATTOO

Express your innermost feelings for a life event or person. Honor a loved one or hero and keep them close by marking your body for life. Placement is critical with memorial tattoos, so decide how much you want the inking to show and the level of pain you can tolerate.

47. NATURE TATTOO

Pay tribute to Mother Nature and invoke feelings of peace and tranquility with designs, including animals, flowers, trees, beaches, and mountains. If you're a man with hobbies like swimming, hiking, mountaineering, and more, then it's time to explore these environmentally-inspired tattoos for men.

48. REALISTIC TATTOO

This technique is all about bringing an image to life. Whether you want the portrait of a loved one, celebrity, or an object that's important to you, you'll need an experienced tattoo artist. Get this right, and you'll have a tattoo for men with profound personal meaning.

49. ROMAN NUMERAL TATTOO

Is there a date that you always want to remember? Roman numeral tattoos are an elegant and unique way to commemorate a special occasion. Thanks to their ability to be scaled up or down to fit anywhere on the body, they are a versatile tattoo idea for men.

50. STICK AND POKE TATTOO

Stick and poke tattoos are on-trend. Swapping a classic electric gun for a hand-held needle and rod-like gadget, the finished result is artistically imperfect and one-of-a-kind. Rebellious and far from mainstream, stick and poke tattoos for men tend to be smaller in size. You can scale them up, though, to suit larger pieces.

51. TRADITIONAL TATTOO

It may have taken the Western world longer to embrace tattoos, but the trend quickly spread once rum-drinking sailors began inking themselves. From those early pioneer days, these old-school tattoos have stood the test of time. Thick, black outlines and bright, bold colors make these traditional tattoos for men design classics.

52. TRIBAL TATTOO

Ancient tribes would use tattoos as protective symbols to either display their social status or as a form of expression. Tribal tattoos for men often feature thick black lines in repeating patterns. They look great large, so the chest, arm, back, and thigh are impressive placements for a well-toned body.

53. RELIGIOUS TATTOO

From Buddhism to Christianity, religious tattoo designs are highly personal and hold a spiritual significance to their owner. They are an impactful tattoo idea for men who want to share their beliefs with the world.

54. POT LEAF TATTOO

A symbol of freedom, marijuana leaf tattoos are tattoos for men who don't conform or give in to social convention. If you want to let the world know that you live life on your terms, this inking will get the message across.

55. ACE TATTOO

Ace cards are the most powerful in the pack. And ace tattoos are a way to show the world you're one of life's winners. They can also symbolize the desire to get a winning hand. A black-inked ace card makes a cool tattoo for men, whatever the motivation.

56. AFRICAN TATTOO

Determination and endurance, this tattoo shows the world you have a place within your chosen people. Traditional African designs are permanent and highly symbolic inking. If you're looking for a cool tattoo for men and want to pay homage to your heritage, your skin is the perfect canvas.

57. BOTANICAL TATTOO

Plant tattoo designs are cool tattoos for men who are at one with nature. From full sleeves to chest and back pieces, they make a creative inking. Better still, there are a lot of manly designs to choose from.

58. HIPSTER TATTOO

It's time to show everyone just how unique you are and wear your hipster tats with pride. Express your originality and get creative with this cool tattoo idea for men. Choose an object or symbol with a special meaning that only you and a handful of others will connect with. This style of tattoo is anything but mainstream! Pair it with a hipster watch brand to show everyone how alternative you are.

59. SEASHELL TATTOO

Seashell tattoos are an original form of body art and make thoughtful tattoos for men who love the sea. But dive that little bit deeper, and you'll discover they're meaningful designs symbolizing love. Show your protection of others around you or shield yourself from negative forces; either way, let your tattoo do the talking.

60. SOBRIETY TATTOO

Sobriety is a long but worthwhile journey. Those following the path may choose a tattoo representing their decision to lead a clean lifestyle and provide constant motivation. The Serenity Prayer, triangle symbol, and coin are all metaphors synonymous with Alcoholics Anonymous. These are popular tattoos for men leading a sober lifestyle.

61. SOUL TATTOO

A soul tattoo is perfect for anyone wanting a holistic inking experience. It often begins with a meditation session and body reading to find out which areas need healing. After this, there may be a tarot reading. The tattoo artist creates a design based on their findings to make meaningful tattoos for men with deep spiritual connections.

62. STONER TATTOO

If getting blazed is one of your favorite pastimes and you don't take life too seriously, why not consider a stoner tattoo? Stoner tattoos for men can be small, large, whimsical, and colorful. Break the mold and get some skin in the game!

63. GOTHIC TATTOO

Skulls, vampires, coffins, bats, and more, symbols of this kind, have a considerable following. Mysterious and brooding, gothic designs are perfect tattoos for men who dabble in the dark arts. Primarily designed in black ink with other rich colors, they're freaky pieces of body art!

64. MOTORCYCLE TATTOO

Wings, eagles, flames, skulls, motorcycle brand names, and club affiliations are just some of the coolest motorcycle tattoos for men. Rarely concealed, and the best bad boy look for half sleeves, full sleeves, and larger body placements, this will go perfectly with a leather jacket.

65. WORLD OF WARCRAFT TATTOO

In 2004 the release of World of Warcraft took the gaming universe by storm, creating over 100 million accounts. Are you a die-hard WoW fan and looking for a cool tattoo idea for men? Get some skin in the game and recreate a permanent shrine to the realm of Azeroth with a mythological character inking.

66. ALPHA AND OMEGA TATTOO

Alpha and Omega may very well be frat houses, but foremost they're the first and last letters of the Greek alphabet. Alpha represents the spiritual essence of a person's existence, while Omega stands for the physical. When inked together, the letters bridge the gap between the soul and body. Both letters combined in a Greek key design can create head-turning tattoos for men.

67. ANARCHY SYMBOL TATTOO

If you have plenty to say about freedom and are fighting for a life free of government control, this bold, black-inking is for you. For hundreds of years, the letter "A" featured inside a circle has symbolized anarchy. These tattoos for men are perfect for anyone wanting to make a political statement.

68. ANIME TATTOO

From romantic to erotic, horrific to comedic, Japanese anime characters are as diverse as their hardcore fans. They're cool tattoos for men who want to showcase their love for this cartoon genre. Bright and bold, decide upon the style that you're looking for and find a skilled artist to bring your idea to life.

69. AVIATION TATTOO

An airplane is a cool tattoo for men who work within the aeronautic industry. For anyone that needs to conceal their inking, perfect placements include the chest, back, ribs, or legs. Better yet, if you have nothing to hide and you enjoy adventure and travel, the sky's the limit! Add on aviator sunglasses and a pilot watch and you'll be ready to hit the tarmac.

70. AZTEC TATTOO

Tattoos to the Aztecs were empowering and symbolized a prosperous life. Each design showed the wearer's warrior status. Aztec tattoos for men are nearly always black and gray but also work well in 3D. Rugged and manly, Aztec tattoos are ideal for showing off a well-worked-out body.

71. CHINESE TATTOO

Chinese history and culture continue to be a source of inspiration for those going under the gun. Chinese letters are no longer trending, but classic, colorful, and bold designs such as the Koi carp and mystical dragon are still popular Chinese tattoos for men.

72. COWBOY TATTOO

Saddle up with a cowboy tattoo to symbolize independence, freedom, strength, and nostalgia for the Wild West. These tattoos for men are a classic choice of ink for anyone interested in cowboy or Western style. What's more, they will never go out of fashion.

73. MAYAN TATTOO

Mayan tattoos are mind-blowing! Intricate, detailed, and show-stopping, they are truly inspirational tattoos for men. The Mayans held their traditions and culture in high regard. Stand out from the crowd and release your inner warrior with an all-black ink, full-sleeve, or full neck.

74. PATRIOTIC TATTOO

Patriotic tattoos for men are an excellent way to honor a specific date in history, happy or sad. They are strong symbols of grief, anger, courage, hope, glory, and resilience. So whether you wear a Celtic-style American flag on your chest or a 3D bald eagle on your back, celebrate history and heritage.

75. SANSKRIT TATTOO

Shanti, which means inner peace, is a popular Sanskrit tattoo design. Another Sanskrit symbol is the all-seeing eye which is a mystical-looking inking with symbolic skin appeal. Both are cool tattoos for men. But, if these don't bring you inner peace and light, why not follow in the footsteps of celeb Russell Brand, who has Anugachhatu Pravah (Go with the Flow) inked on his right arm?

76. SPORTS TATTOO

From basketball to baseball, boxing to biking, and beyond, sports tattoos for men are a permanent way to show your support for a particular activity, player, or team. So get your game on with a portrait, sportswear brand or team logo, or name, and wear your fan favorite with pride!

77. FINGERPRINT TATTOO

Every man has his markings making a fingerprint tattoo the most unique skin inking ever! The best placement for these types of tattoos for men is on an area of skin that won't stretch or quickly age. These include the feet, ankles, or shoulder. For new dads, they're a special way to mark a birth.

78. HOURGLASS TATTOO

Mark your body and the passage of time with an hourglass tattoo. Choose a black and gray design for a vintage vibe, or give your hourglass wings to symbolize time flying by. For something more abstract, a Dali-esque hourglass is a reminder of time slipping away. A symbol of patience and a reminder of mortality, there are lots of cool tattoo ideas for men just waiting for a suitable canvas!

79. LATIN TATTOO

Language of the ancient Romans, there are hundreds of badass Latin sayings to suit any mood. For Alpha males who prefer to lead than follow, "Non-Ducor, Duco" (I am not led, I lead) is a powerful choice. If you've overcome a challenging personal situation and are looking for a cool tattoo idea for men? "Ad Astra per Astra" (Through Adversity to the Stars) is a meaningful reminder of what you can achieve.

80. PORTRAIT TATTOO

Portrait tattoos are a way to carry a loved one close. However, portrait tattoos for men can also pay tribute to a role model or inspirational celebrity. For the best results, find a tattoo artist specializing in portrait work as designs are sometimes 3D and require an artistic eye and a lot of skill.

81. MATCHING TATTOO

Matching tattoos are not only for couples. Strong bonds between friends, siblings, and family can strengthen thanks to matching body art. Complementary tats can either be identical or two halves that make a whole. The size, style, and design options are limitless, making matching designs one of the most fun tattoo ideas for men.

82. ANCHOR TATTOO

Anchor tattoos have, for centuries, carried multiple meanings. To sailors or those who work at sea, they represent stability. In Christianity, the anchor represented Christians trying to escape Roman persecution. For others, the anchor may symbolize love for the ocean. Anchor tattoos for men needn't be retro; combine them with other nautical styles for a modern interpretation.

83. BROTHER TATTOO

A brotherly bond is like no other. A supporter and confidant who has your unwavering trust, brothers aren't always connected by genes. Some are of the heart, not blood. So what better way to celebrate a special relationship than with matching ink? Cement your bond of brotherhood and embrace your sensitive side with these cool tattoos for men.

84. DREAMCATCHER TATTOO

A dreamcatcher catches bad dreams while only allowing good dreams to pass through. If you're looking for a calm and sound night's sleep, no need to count sheep. Instead, opt for one of these cool tattoos for men, and catch those z's.

85. EARTH TATTOO

The symbol of life and the manifestation of home, earth tattoos for men can work well, big or small. Some get this inking to represent their passion for travel, while others want to show their gratitude to Mother Earth. If you feel like you carry the weight of the world, wear this tattoo on the shoulder or back!

86. JOKER TATTOO

Thank Batman for this cool tattoo idea for men! Since the character's TV debut in 1966, the Joker continues to be a timeless inking. Just like his on-screen persona, Joker's tattoos represent life's darker side. Meanwhile, joker playing card tattoos symbolize good luck but can also represent misfortune and deceit. If you're a free-spirited guy of extremes, it's the wild card you're looking for!

87. SEMICOLON TATTOO

This simple punctuation mark is a symbol of solidarity and hope for anyone battling mental health issues. They constantly remind a story is yet to be completed and inspire their wearer to look towards the future. These meaningful tattoos for men look good inked anywhere on the body.

88. WAVE TATTOO

A wave tattoo is a symbol of strength and the perseverance to reach a final destination. Waves also make cool tattoos for men who love surfing and adventure. If you're looking for a small tattoo on the wrist or a large inking on the arm or back, it's time to hit the waves!

89. BUDDHA TATTOO

Buddha is one of the key symbols of the Buddhist religion. His image and teachings are about understanding, wisdom, and enlightenment. Many artistic interpretations of Buddha exist. Before embarking on any religious-themed inking, take time to research and make sure your chosen tattoo design for men isn't insensitive to followers of that religion.

90. EYE TATTOO

The eye is significant in many different cultures. In Greece, an evil eye is a bitter look capable of cursing someone, and a blue eye, or mati, pendant protects its wearer from such a curse. In India, the third eye is a chakra, which, when opened, increases intuition and wisdom. In any case, this is one eye-catching tattoo for men!

91. HEART TATTOO

This tattoo is for the man who wears his heart on his sleeve. A symbol of life, love, and sometimes loss, heart tattoos are for those not afraid to show their sensitive side. Heart tattoos for men often incorporate contrasting design elements to give a more masculine vibe.

92. INFINITY TATTOO

Initially used in mathematics to signify the concept of limitlessness, the infinity symbol has since developed a more spiritual meaning. It is now a representation of everlasting love or endless possibilities. Infinity, which looks like a figure of eight on its side, is ideal for small body areas. Let this small tattoo for men take you to infinity and beyond!

93. KOI FISH TATTOO

The color of a Koi fish tattoo changes its meaning. Orange/yellow fish bring prosperity and fortune. A black Koi symbolizes overcoming a life struggle, and the redfish represents bravery and strength. For peace and fertility, choose a blue inking. And if you desire career success, choose a white fish. Whatever color you choose, though, even if that's black and gray, Koi fish tattoos for men are steeped in historical meaning.

94. MEANINGFUL TATTOO

Meaningful tattoos are personal to their owner and carry sentimental value. Meaningful tattoos for men are truly unique, and the design and style reflect what's important to their wearer. That may be a date, a memorial to a lost loved one, or a symbol that inspires to make it through tough times.

95. MEXICAN TATTOO

Mexico is the land of the Aztecs, with stunning nature, rich tradition, and the best margaritas. There's no doubt, that Mexico is bursting with culture and beauty. So share the love and honor your heritage with a Mexican-inspired tattoo for men. Wear your patriotic tattoo with pride, somewhere the world can see, such as the arm or leg.

96. MINIMALIST TATTOO

Go back to basics with a minimalistic tattoo. Straight lines, little detail, and limited shading, minimalistic tattoos for men are the epitome of understated cool. Just because they follow strict design aesthetics doesn't mean you can't get creative. What's more, they take less time to ink, so are less expensive than most other designs and will suit any minimalist wardrobe with ease.

97. MOM TATTOO

Mom is the most important woman in a man's life. When thinking of a mom tattoo, the image that probably comes to mind is an American-traditional design with a bold red heart and white "mom" banner. While these Sailor Jerry retro inkings are still popular today, mom tattoos for men can also take a more sentimental approach.

98. SPIRITUAL TATTOO

Spirituality means different things to many people. Celtic knots, Yin and Yang, the lotus, mandala, third eye, or hamsa may be symbols that resonate with you. On the other hand, maybe your spirituality is not so easily defined and is better represented with a more abstract, personalized design. Regardless, spiritual tattoos for men tell a story. What that story is, though, is yours to tell.

99. SUN TATTOO

Truth and light are two of the common meanings for this type of tattoo. They are a symbol of powering through dark and challenging times and reaching the light. The sun is one of the most revered symbols throughout the world. Shine a light on your skin with sun tattoos for men.

100. WATERCOLOR TATTOO

Watercolor tattoos are vivid and bright with subtle color gradients and techniques to create the look of a classic watercolor painting. They need fewer skin punctures, so are less painful. Break the rules and express your art with these conversation-starting tattoos for men.

101. BUTTERFLY TATTOO

A butterfly tattoo is the symbol of balance following transformation. These creatures combine physical and spiritual beauty to create sensual tattoos for men representing freedom, courage, accomplishment, and rebirth. For men who have earned their wings, it's a statement tattoo for the arms, shins, chest, back, or hands.

102. BEST FRIENDS TATTOO

Best friends are the family we choose. Matching or complementary ink makes that connection everlasting. Get together and agree on your shared interests and aesthetics. If your bud wants to go large, but you need an easy-to-conceal tattoo for men, find a design that looks good in different sizes and places. Remember, best friends, just like tattoos, are forever.

103. DISNEY TATTOO

Whimsical and fun, Disney tattoos are sure to have a place in your heart. This genre of tattoos for men will make sure you keep a lifelong connection with your precious memories. Embrace your inner child, choose your favorite character or movie, and get a magical inking.

104. DOG TATTOO

Dogs can often be our closest and most loyal companions. Whether you want to honor the breed in general or pay homage to a particular pet, dog tattoos for men are a way to celebrate your K-9 connection.

105. FOOD TATTOO

Food tattoos are often colorful, fun, and sometimes whimsical. Whether a chef or a foodie, food-themed designs are a cool tattoo for men who want to take a more relaxed and entertaining approach to their body art and their love for food trends.

106. SNAKE TATTOO

Wrap or coil this design around the object of your desire, be it a skull, wild animal, flower, or person. Snakes shed their skins and so are often a symbol of transformation, rebirth, and change. Snake tattoos for men are versatile, easy to customize and make popular tattoos for arms and muscular parts of the body.

107. MAZE TATTOO

In Greek mythology, the maze, designed by Dedalus, was a means to enslave the fearsome Minotaur beast beneath Knossos Palace. Each year, until the hero Theseus, came to defeat the beast, children got sent to the maze as sacrifices. Theseus escaped the maze using a piece of the red string given to him by Princess Ariadne. Maze tattoos for men will guarantee you always have an incredible story to tell.

108. MOON TATTOO

Full moon, crescent moon, total eclipse; the moon's phases control the Earth's tides. Spiritually, the moon symbolizes eternity, immortality, and enlightenment. It's no wonder it also has links to mythological creatures such as werewolves and witches. Moon tattoos for men can vary from realistic illustrations to mystical artworks.

109. PRAYING HANDS TATTOO

Praying hands are a symbol within Christianity but are also associated with Hinduism, Judaism, and Buddhism. Their meaning is one of sincerity, dedication, and respect for a Higher Power. Praying hands are a cool tattoo idea for men who are either spiritual or religious.

110. ROOTS TATTOO

Connect to the past and choose a tattoo for men to symbolize ancestry, physical health, and spiritual growth. While black and gray ink captures the allure of tree root designs, earthy tones work well too. Depending on the design's size and style, suitable placements include the forearm, bicep, chest, back, and ribs.

111. CAMPING TATTOO

Tattoos for men relating to life under the stars and escaping from the humdrum of everyday city life are sick! Explore designs of campfires, trees, mountains, rivers, and sunsets. Symbolic, photographic, tribal, cartoon-like, or realistic but never dull! These are the best-ever tattoos for men who are wild at heart!

112. PHOENIX TATTOO

The mystical phoenix is a symbol of birth, death, and rebirth. It can mark its wearer as facing hardship and turmoil before turning over a new leaf and getting stronger. Rise above the ashes and check out the many impressive phoenix tattoo designs for men.

113. ELEPHANT TATTOO

An elephant never forgets, and when you choose this magnificent beast as a permanent skin marking, you'll have an unforgettable tattoo for men. Symbolizing love, loyalty, strength, family, and good luck, this giant of the jungle is a powerful inking. Treat your body like a temple and showcase an incredible elephant tattoo.

114. HONEYCOMB TATTOO

Honeycomb tattoo designs for men are complex and a symbol of male mystique. Honeycombs are one of the most amazing designs in nature and a testament that with hard work, it's possible to achieve your goals. These geometrically challenging designs make an impressive full-body tattoo that will get everyone buzzing.

115. IRISH TATTOO

The Celtic people can trace their origins back before modern civilization and take credit for making Irish society and culture what it is today. Honor your roots with a Celtic tattoo for men. The most popular choices are a Celtic cross, knot, or harp.

116. MAP TATTOO

Map tattoos are an artistic way to commemorate a connection to a stylish destination or passion for travel. If you've backpacked around the world or travel is top of your wish list, celebrate your wanderlust with a map tattoo for men.

117. VIKING TATTOO

Popular on-screen, Vikings are well-loved warriors. There are many Viking tattoo designs to choose from. There's the Helm of Awe, for protection and power, Thor's Hammer to instill courage, protection, and generosity, and Vegvisir, or the pathfinder, a compass to guide its wearer home. Release your inner Ragnor Lodbrok and check out these cool tattoos for men!

118. SHADOW TATTOO

Go over to the dark side with deep, inky, and mysterious designs. Shadow tattoos for men feature heavy shading for an ink that is eye-catching and bold. They are the most impactful for gothic and spooky designs.

119. UNALOME TATTOO

In Buddhism, the unwelcome symbol represents the path to enlightenment. Its spirals, for men, face inwards and symbolize the twist and turns we experience in life. Its lines straighten the moment we achieve peace, harmony, or enlightenment, and the dots, many believe, mean death. Popular with men who are into yoga classes and devotees alike, it's a tattoo for anyone wanting to achieve happiness and inner peace.

120. ZEN TATTOO

Enzo is a sacred Zen Buddhism symbol that means a circle of togetherness. It represents elegance, strength, and one-mindedness. Ideal placements for this rounded design are the shoulder or chest. The circle may be one of the more simple tattoos for men, but it has deep meaning for its wearers.

121. MANDALA TATTOO

Hinduism and Buddhism use the mandala as a symbol to represent the universe and spiritual journey. Round in shape, mandalas are like snowflakes in that each one is unique. Their repeating patterns make mandalas highly customizable tattoos for men. Wrap around the wrist in a cuff, encircle the elbow, or place the tattoo on the nape of the neck.

Chapter 6

100 BEST TATTOO IDEAS FOR WOMEN

The Best Tattoo Ideas For Women

Tattoos are so on-trend, but you want them to either have a special meaning or to be creative. It can be hard deciding what to get. After all, it's going to be there for the rest of your life (unless you get it lasered), therefore, placement is also a big consideration. Just to help you out, we've put together the best tattoo ideas for women and some advice to guide you through the process.

1. Butterfly Tattoos

If you're looking for inspiration for fresh new ink, you may want to consider a butterfly. Although butterfly tattoos have been popular for decades, there is a timelessness about them, and the wide variety of designs has ensured that each piece remains unique to the wearer. Butterflies can be delicate and beautiful, but they can also represent transformation, resilience, hope, and even love. There is also a feminine element to the design, which is why it is such a popular choice among women.

2. Dragon Tattoos

Dragon tattoos can make a powerful statement, and they symbolize wisdom, fearlessness, and protection. The stories of these mythical beasts are found in many cultures around the world. They have featured heavily in both European mythologies, as well as in East Asian cultures. Often, a dragon is considered to be a fierce and powerful creature, something to be respected, but also feared. When deciding to get a tattoo, you can draw from the many inspirations and interpretations, but ultimately choose what you want the ink to represent to you; whether that be passion or mystery, or something more profound.

3. Lion Tattoos

The lion is considered the ruler of the animal kingdom, or the king of the jungle, and it is a creature that is both well respected and feared. When deciding to ink this powerful predator, many people choose to do so because of the traits associated with it; courage, bravery, royalty, and wisdom. There are many variations of the lion tattoo design, with some individuals opting for a super realistic approach, and others choosing to combine various elements, such as flowers and shapes, to create a unique and more feminine finish.

4. Semicolon Tattoos

Tattoos can have deeply personal meanings, and the semicolon tattoo design is one of them. It has become a symbol for those suffering from mental health and depression and reminds the wearer that their story is not over yet. Their journey has not come to an end, and their lives will continue, despite their struggles. It is for this reason that these tattoos work best in places where they can easily be seen, like on the wrist, so that they can serve as a daily reminder of the obstacles that the individual has overcome and how they are capable of dealing with them in the future.

5. Wolf Tattoos

If you want to ink something that represents love and loyalty, then consider a wolf tattoo. These beautiful animals live in packs, and their strength and survival depend on their numbers. It is for this reason that this design often symbolizes family, suggesting there is power in unity, and it encourages the wearer to remember the importance of these close familial bonds. The wolf also has special significance to specific cultures, namely the Native Americans, who have a deep respect for the animal.

6. Elephant Tattoos

Elephants are majestic animals, and they also represent power and prosperity. These gigantic mammals are often associated with fantastic memory; you may have heard the saying "an elephant never forgets," which is why they also symbolize wisdom. What you may not know is that the head of an elephant herd is always a female, and thus, this can be a fantastic piece for a woman who wants to celebrate her femininity. You can choose a large, intricate elephant tattoo design, or something small and simple, the great thing about this ink is it works in a variety of sizes.

7. Scorpion Tattoos

If you want a more edgy tattoo, the scorpion is an excellent choice. These predatory arachnids are often considered to be dangerous because of their ability to inflict pain, and those who choose a symbol like this often want it to serve as a warning. The design can be incredibly powerful and a show of strength and intimidation. It can also remind the wearer of the need to protect themselves from those who want to cause them harm.

8. Snake Tattoos

Snake tattoos represent many different things; for some, they are considered to be evil creatures, for example, in the Christian Bible story of Adam and Eve, the snake was the tempter and resulted in sin. However, for others, they are mythical and powerful. A Japanese snake tattoo can represent strength, protection, and even good luck, and in Native American cultures, the rattlesnake is of great importance. Another trait associated with serpent ink is the idea of transformation or rebirth because snakes shed their skin. They can also symbolize danger or fertility.

9. Heart Tattoos

The heart is one of the most popular tattoo choices, and for a good reason. It is a universally recognized symbol across all cultures and holds deep meaning for the wearer, including love, loss, and heartbreak. Individuals can choose from a wide range of heart tattoo designs, some simple, like an outline, and others more detailed, like a sacred heart. Color also plays an important role when choosing what is right for you; for example, red ink can celebrate friendship and love, while black represents sorrow.

10. Skull Tattoos

Skull tattoos are often intricate and take time and skill to complete. It is a recognizable image across many cultures and is typically associated with death or mortality. These pieces can take on a wide range of meanings, depending on the design, and have remained a popular choice of ink for decades. If you are looking for a way to make the tattoo more feminine, consider bold colors or floral details. Regardless of what you choose, though, there is no denying your ink will stand out.

11. Watercolour Tattoos

Standard black ink works well for some designs, but if you want something more daring, you will love watercolor tattoos. The style is relatively new, although it is quickly gaining popularity, and the technique creates a finish that looks as though someone has expertly painted a masterpiece onto your skin. Many designs lend themselves well to watercolors, but flowers tend to be the most popular, creating a bold, vibrant finish. Tattoos like this work exceptionally well when combined with a black base, which helps to keep the ink from fading quickly and creates a more recognizable outline.

12. Angel Tattoos

Tattoos can represent sorrow and warn about danger, or they could be uplifting and inspiring, like an angel design. Angels are associated with heaven and are seen as pure beings, determined to protect all that is good and sacred. For this reason, these tattoos can be a fantastic choice for those who are religious and want to honor their faith. Alternatively, they can serve as a tribute to a loved one, or as a reminder that the wearer has a guardian watching over them.

13. Compass Tattoos

If you are a passionate traveler and want a design that inspires direction, then look no further than a compass tattoo. The symbolism dates back to sailors, who are believed to have inked their skin with these images to help them navigate while at sea, and it is for this reason that these designs often represent guidance and protection. When choosing a compass tattoo, the wearer may also want to remind themselves of the hard times that they have overcome; the navigational instrument can guide you through rough patches and help you to remember where you're going in life.

14. Sun Tattoos

Without the sun, we would not be able to survive. It is a source of light and energy but can represent the truth, or serve as a symbol of hope; someone has overcome a dark period in their lives and found a way out of it. Others may be inspired by the sun because it reminds them of the beauty of life. There are many sun tattoo designs, and their meaning can be somewhat ambiguous, allowing the wearer to customize their ink to suit their personal preference.

15. Clock Tattoos

Time is a precious commodity, and we are all living each day on earth, not knowing when our time will be up. It is for this reason that clock tattoos often represent the balance between life and death. Individuals can tailor their ink to make it unique and personal; some of the ways this can be done is by including flowers, to honor the living. Alternatively, you could take a darker approach by adding skulls or fire. The position where the hands of the timepiece have stopped can make the piece even more personal.

16. Crown Tattoos

When you think of a crown, images of royalty will automatically come to mind, but that's not all that this tattoo can represent. The design can have powerful symbolism, with typical attributes including victory, self-control, and authority. A woman who chooses to get a crown tattoo on her skin may feel she wields her destiny, or that she demands respect and equality. In terms of placement, crown tattoos are incredibly versatile. They work well as small designs and outlines, which can be inked onto the wrist, but also as bigger, more detailed pieces on the forearm or thigh.

17. Dream Catcher Tattoos

Individuals who want a meaningful tattoo should consider this beautiful piece. A dreamcatcher, originally a hand-woven product that is meant to replicate a spider's web, has roots in Native American culture. It is a symbol of protection, hung to guard against evil thoughts, and a way of filtering out the negative experiences to focus on the good. A dream catcher tattoo is often incredibly detailed, and because of this, it tends to work better on larger areas of skin, with the thigh being a popular choice.

18. Eye Tattoos

When you think of an eye, the gift of sight comes to mind, right? Well, this is the fundamental concept of the eye tattoo. The eye can symbolize something that is all-seeing; for example, in Christianity, it can represent God watching over you.

Alternatively, it could be interpreted as a symbol of guidance or protection. There are many different choices with regards to the placement of this design; you can choose to go small and ink it onto your finger or opt for a more detailed piece on your thigh.

19. Bird Tattoos

Many people dream of having wings and being able to fly away from their troubles, and bird tattoos are a way of showing that. These beautiful winged creatures symbolize many things, including freedom and independence. They can also serve as a reminder that we do not need to adhere to certain earthly constraints. There are many different bird designs; for example, a raven could represent death, while a goldfinch or canary are species that are typically associated with happiness.

20. Henna Tattoos

Getting a tattoo is not a decision that should be made overnight because it is meant to be a piece that will be with you forever. Many people think long and hard before choosing a design that is meaningful to them, but if you are not ready for a long-term commitment, you may want to consider something more temporary, like a henna tattoo. It is created using a plant-based dye, and these intricate pieces can be made using various shades, including red, orange, brown, and blue-black. Henna is popular at Indian weddings or festivals and is known as mehndi, but it is also traditional in Morocco and Egypt. Another pro to this form of tattooing is that the dye fades naturally over time.

21. Unique Tattoos

Depending on the person, unique tattoos can vary. A unique tattoo can be something personal or some sort of interesting design. Whatever it is, this kind of tattoo is probably going to be special to you, or may even be a conversation starter.

22. Cute Little Tattoos

Who said your tattoo had to be huge? As long as you find an artist who specializes in small designs, you can easily get something rather detailed, in a much smaller, cuter version. Little dainty tattoos are always a good idea if you're wanting a tattoo but aren't looking for something too bold and noticeable.

23. Small tattoos

Small tattoos are generally kept quite conservative and simple. They don't take more than ten to twenty minutes to get done depending on the style. Though just because it's small, that doesn't mean you can't make it personal.

24. Cross Tattoos

Cross tattoos can be as simple as two lines or two words in cursive, intersecting. If you want to get more creative, you could add something wrapped around it, such as a flower design. They're a great choice if you have a religious background and it gives you the option of intertwining two ideas into one design.

25. Simple Tattoos

Simple tattoos are normally something like a heart, a moon, the sun, or the basic outline of a flower or animal. They're a great choice if you're struggling to come up with a design. Usually, you can explain to your artist what you're after, and they'll show you an option very quickly of something they may have already stenciled up.

26. Flower Tattoos

Flower tattoos are very popular for women, especially wildflowers. This doesn't mean you can't think outside of the box and create your ideas though. There are so many different types of flowers to choose from. You could get anything from the outline of lavender to a water lily sitting on a pad.

27. Hand Tattoos

There is so much you can insinuate with hand tattoos, such as love, peace, and promises. They're usually just an outline but you can make them as bold and detailed as you like.

28. Lettering Tattoos

Lettering tattoos are great if you have a famous quote that you love or a saying that resonates with you. These tattoos usually look rather delicate depending on the style of font you go with.

29. Stick and Poke Tattoos

Stick and poke tattoos are enjoying a surge of popularity in recent years. This is because people look for alternative styles and ways to ink themselves; it is worth noting that the DIY approach is not recommended. That said, it is one of the oldest methods for body art. The technique uses a needle and rod-type contraption and is inked by hand instead of with an electric tattoo machine. The result is unique, with each piece having slight imperfections and a very distinct appearance, but that is the beauty of this style. It may also be appealing to a woman who wants something that has a rebellious association or wishes to get back to the basics of tattooing in its original form. When it comes to what you can get inked, there are no limits, from small to big pieces.

30. Minimalist Tattoos

Body art doesn't have to be extremely detailed to make a statement, as the minimalist tattoo trend shows. They are often created using black lines, and minimal color, and it simplifies the design. The great thing about this technique is it focuses more on the subject matter rather than the style used to create it. It will often be devoid of shading and created using crisp, clean lines. There is no limit to what you can or cannot get done, but most people opt for something small or basic, which is great if you are looking for a delicate piece or something discreet and can be covered up easily. Pick something filled with meaning that inspires your daily life or a symbol you love.

31. 3D Tattoos

The art of tattooing is so fantastic because there are so many different styles to choose from. Undoubtedly one of the most eye-catching and detailed is the 3D tattoo, which, as the name suggests, adds an extra dimension to your artwork to make it look as though your design has come to life on your skin. The use of shadows, shading, and blur creates the illusion of depth. The skill of your chosen tattoo artist will allow you to pick from a wide variety of images, but some of the most popular choices are things like butterflies or dragonflies, which can be created to look as though they are hovering above you. Another popular approach is to make it appear as though your design is within your skin. For example, a flag from your country to show your patriotism or a robotic design for a futuristic feel.

32. Sibling Tattoos

What better way to celebrate the bond you share with your family than with a sibling tattoo? The relationship between siblings is like no other. It is unconditional love, a best friend for life, and someone who will always have your back. Whether you choose to celebrate sisterhood or the close relationship you have with your brother, many great designs choose from reflecting this. Maybe you want a gender-neutral image or matching pieces? Or choose to celebrate a memory from childhood with one of your favorite cartoon characters or symbols. They share many choices from simple to detailed, so find something that both you and the sibling love that you will cherish for the rest of your life.

33. Skeleton Hand Tattoos

Some tattoo designs are pretty and delicate, others are cool and terrifying, and the skeleton hand tattoo defines the latter category. This option is for someone who has a rebellious streak and does not want to blend into the crowd because it is visible and makes a statement. The human skeleton is often associated with death, and although this may seem like a very morbid image to get inked, it can represent fearlessness and show that you do not fear what is to come. It is also associated with renewal and impermanence, a reminder to live life to the fullest. In addition to being very symbolic, deciding to get tattooed on your hand is a daring choice. Not only is it an area that is considered high on the tattoo pain chart scale because of the nerve endings and thin skin, but it is also incredibly visible.

34. Japanese Tattoos

Japanese tattoos are a much-loved style because they are bold and bright, as well as extremely expressive. The subject matter is very important and often based on tradition or folklore. Common images include animals, flowers, or mythical beings — for example, tigers and koi fish, the lotus or cherry blossom, and dragons and phoenixes. The colors and shading make these pieces stand out, so it is an excellent option for someone who wants an exciting and eye-catching design. Colors can also alter the meaning of your tat; for example, a black koi fish represents masculinity and adversity, while a green dragon has links to nature. Body art in Japan is shrouded in controversy, and there is a stigma attached to it. This is because of the association with the notorious Yakuza gang, which covers their entire bodies in ink to show their commitment to the organization.

35. Family Tattoos

For many people, their family is their priority. These people will stand by their side through the good times and the bad, show their support, and give their love freely. So, what better way to honor this bond than with a family tattoo? The fantastic thing about getting ink that celebrates your loved ones is that there are many designs to choose from. Some are simple, like a heart, a quote that has special significance to you, or a tiny matching symbol. Other people want something more detailed, like a family tree filled with everyone's names or a crest. There are also certain animals, flowers, and objects that are associated with family. For example, an anchor represents stability, a wolf symbolizes loyalty, teamwork, and protection, and flowers like hydrangeas are often inked to honor family.

36. American Traditional Tattoos

Its bold appearance defines the American Traditional tattoo technique. It uses thick black lines, and a bright but limited color palette of yellow, green, red, and blue, and the pieces often involve a certain theme. Popular choices are animals, nature, humans, and nautical artwork. Your ink can also tell a story by combining several images. These pieces are symbolic and bound to get noticed and make a statement thanks to the interesting subject and approach. If you are not afraid to stand out from the crowd, then this is the choice for you.

37. Arrow Tattoos

If you are unsure of what to get for your next inking, consider an arrow tattoo. The weapon has significance to the Native American people, who used it for hunting, fighting, and protecting themselves, and it is seen as a symbol of strength, resilience, and power. There are many ways to get this piece tattooed, and it suits varying techniques from minimalist to watercolor. Some people choose to include an image of a bow and arrow; others may focus on an arrow compass design; a reminder to stay on the right path and help you find your way. After deciding on a style, consider the placement of your ink. Is it large and detailed? Then the thigh or the shoulder are fantastic options. If you prefer something simple or small, then the wrist, forearm, or behind the ear are all spots women love to get tattooed.

38. Feather Tattoos

Feather tattoos are a popular choice because they are symbolic. In general, a feather is connected to the ideas of freedom, courage, and wisdom. It is the perfect design for a woman who has a free spirit and wants to indicate that she does not follow the rules set out by society. Or it could have a spiritual association, as plumage has played an important part in Native American culture and is used for much more than decorative purposes. The piece looks good in color or black ink and suits a wide variety of styles, from simplistic and minimalistic, to bright options like the watercolor effect. The type of feather you choose to get inked can also say a lot about you. A peacock's plumes, for example, are colorful and bold and represent beauty, pride, royalty, and luxury, while an eagle's feather is associated with bravery and strength.

39. Medusa Tattoos

Medusa represents a monster associated with jealousy and rage, but she symbolizes freedom, transformation, and femininity for others. Regardless of how you choose to interpret the snake-haired maiden, you are likely familiar with her image and maybe even her story; according to Ancient Greek mythology, she was cursed by the goddess Athena, causing anyone who caught her gaze to turn to stone. She became a victim of Athena's rage because of her association with the god, Poseidon. Your Medusa tattoo design can be big or small, simple or hyper-realistic; the choice is yours. The placement of your chosen ink is just as important. Medusa is often seen as a feminist symbol and can be empowering, and you may want to express this by choosing a particularly feminine or sexy part of the body. For example, the thigh.

40. Geometric Tattoos

Geometric tattoos are a great option for focusing on the lines and shapes, thus creating a unique finish. They represent balance, symmetry, harmony, and even mystery. Almost every image can have a geometric element to it, whether you choose to get an animal or a floral design. Thanks to this approach's versatility, you can get something meaningful to you, but it will also be visually interesting. When choosing the perfect spot to get inked, consider the size of your chosen tattoo and whether you want it to be discreet or not. The wrist is a popular spot for women who want to look at their design every day, while the forearm or the thigh allow for bigger, more detailed designs and are easy to cover up.

41. Moon Tattoos

If you want a symbol of transition, creativity, and growth, then a moon tattoo is perfect for you. The earth's natural satellite can be tattooed in one of its phases, including a full, half, or crescent shape, each with different meanings. Perhaps you are drawn to the ideas of magic and mystery; then, a full moon is a fantastic choice as it is associated with the supernatural. The crescent can represent hope and change, and a half-moon is for a woman inspired by creativity or who wants a piece that shows the transitions she's going through in life. It can also be symbolic of growth and attainment. The moon can include various other images, which can alter the meaning of your tattoo. For example, a sun and moon tattoo, which you can view as a coming together of opposites and a representation of two opposing forces.

42. Phoenix Tattoos

The Phoenix is an important symbol of life, death, and rebirth and is a popular image to get tattooed because of its incredible meaning. It has been featured in myths and culture, including Greek mythology and Chinese folklore. The firebird represents hope and perseverance, serving as a reminder that you can rise above whatever you face. It is also associated with renewal because the creature goes through cycles, regenerating by bursting into flames and rising from the ashes of its predecessor. This is an excellent choice for a woman who is going through a difficult period in her life. There are many styles to choose from, whether you want a small, basic outline to something large and extremely detailed. It can be inked in black but looks particularly striking in color. A popular choice is to create your phoenix tattoo using reds and oranges, imitating the appearance of fire.

43. Behind The Ear Tattoos

When it comes to body art, the placement of your piece is often just as important as the subject matter. You want to consider visibility and pain and if the area will suit your chosen design. One of the coolest and most discreet spots is a behind-the-ear tattoo. In recent years they have become extremely popular because they allow for delicate and feminine artwork. It would be best if you opted for small designs, and often keeping them simple is best. Despite not seeing it every day, knowing your inking is etched onto your skin is enough. Be warned that tattooing in this location will hurt and will not hold ink as long as in other areas. That said, you may feel all this is worth it because the result is impressive.

44. Lotus Tattoos

The lotus is not just a visually interesting and beautiful flower but also a symbolic one. A lotus tattoo represents many things, including a balance between the body, mind, and spirit. It is often associated with beauty, strength, and spiritual awakening and is a fantastic choice for a woman who wants to reflect her personal growth or enlightenment. Another common theme involves resilience. The conditions that the lotus grows in, muddy and murky waters, may seem less than ideal. This is often seen as a reminder that hope and goodness are waiting when times are tough. There are many colors to choose from, each with a slightly different meaning. For example, red for matters of the heart and blue for spirituality.

45. Mother and Daughter Tattoos

The bond between a mama and her daughter is hard to describe, but it is one of the purest forms of love. This is the woman that will do anything for you, love you without question, and always support you. What better way to honor this special bond than with a mother and daughter tattoo? Deciding on the perfect design to celebrate each other will likely come easy to you. It can be anything, whether you want matching ink, a piece that complements another, or something completely different but with unique symbolism. A few choices include phrases like 'mama' and 'mama's girl.' Or it could be of mother and child characters or matching symbols such as hearts or flowers. Your body art doesn't have to be large or detailed to be meaningful, but you may want to opt for a placement where you can see your cat every day.

46. Rose Tattoos

One of the most popular and frequently inked images is a rose. A rose tattoo is not only beautiful but also symbolic. The bloom represents life, beauty, and pain and that some things are not always what they seem; the flower is stunning, but the thorns cause pain. This can be a reminder to keep your heart guarded or be wary of who you trust. The color you choose will also alter the meaning of your design. Red is associated with passion, love, and even anger, while yellow is the hue that represents friendship and joy. It is also common to combine the rose with various images, such as a serpent, skull, or heart. Think about the meaning you want and the image you wish to convey to find the perfect look for you.

47. Matching Couple Tattoos

When you think you have found the one, you may want to celebrate your connection with a matching couple tattoo. Deciding to honor someone with your body art is a big decision, and this will make a statement about your relationship and your dedication to it. It is a way to join you together for life. When it comes to finding the perfect artwork, this can be anything. Maybe you love the same character from a book or game, or perhaps there is a quote that moves you. It could also be two complementary images, for example, a lock and a key, or words that show you're taken. Or an inside joke that has to mean only the two you understand. Deciding to get inked together is also a bonding experience and a memory you will cherish forever.

48. Sunflower Tattoos

A sunflower tattoo symbolizes hope, optimism, everlasting love, and adoration. It is associated with the sun and represents happiness; just looking at them can fill you with joy and bring a smile to your face. The meaning behind these flowers makes them a popular option for women who want to remind themselves to look on the bright side of life. It is a piece that can be inked in various places. This includes visible options like the wrist to more discreet areas like the thigh. One of the most beautfíful things about a sunflower is, of course, its color, and deciding to get it inked in bright yellow will make a statement. That said, a black ink piece or a simple outline still has the same meaning.

49. Sister Tattoos

The relationship between sisters is special. She may be your best friend and the person to who you tell all your secrets, and you will always be there for each other. Sister tattoos are a wonderful way to celebrate your connection and an opportunity to show each other and the rest of the world how much they mean to you. They can be matching, complementary pieces, or tell a story. Maybe you want artwork that reminds you of something from your childhood or a cute animal that you both love. Quotes, words, and dates are also meaningful options. You can get them tattooed in the same spot or in different places; it is the symbolism associated with your ink that counts. Coming up with the design you will get inked will be half the fun, so get brainstorming.

50. Best Friend Tattoos

Celebrating the bond you share with your family is important, but some friends in your life are also family, even if not related by blood. Best friend tattoos are an excellent choice to get inked to honor the relationship with the person who always has your back. Maybe you met as children on the first day of school, or perhaps you have grown up together since you were babies, and if so, you want to get inked with a memory from childhood. Other options include matching pieces, which could be of anything meaningful to you and your bestie. Quotes can represent your relationship; friendship symbols, small birds, tiny hearts, and infinity signs are cute options.

51. Wings Tattoo

A wings tattoo is a fantastic choice for a woman who wants a piece associated with freedom and change. Freedom can mean many things, whether it is to free yourself of the darkness that haunts your past or to open your mind up to new things, so it is not hard to see why someone would be drawn to this idea. There are also various ways to design your wings, and they can resemble bird feathers or angel wings. Opting for the latter can also be symbolic of protection, faith, and direction. It could honor a loved one who has passed or serve as a reminder that there is goodness in your life.

52. Badass Tattoo

Do you want body art that can be intimidating or help make you look tough and cool? Then look no further than a badass tattoo. What you get inked depends on your personality and the style you're drawn to, but it is more about expressing yourself and making a statement than anything else. Some women opt for snakes or scorpions, getting them inked in a 3D technique to let them come to life on the skin. Others may be drawn to a robotic or futuristic tattoo which can be scary yet awesome. Another option may be to try out a Viking-inspired design, as these formidable warriors were often associated with power, strength, and fearlessness. The choice is yours, so let your creativity guide you.

53. Sun and Moon Tattoos

A sun and moon tattoo is more than just a pretty design; it is also symbolic. The combination is associated with family, mystery, femininity, hope, and guidance. It can be linked to opposites, such as good and bad and light and dark. This is an excellent choice for someone who wishes to remind themselves that there is light to be found in the darkness. Some women also wish to honor their familial bonds with this piece, and the stars can represent your children or family members. The number can correlate to how many are in your family.

54. Meaningful Tattoo

Body art is a wonderful way to express yourself and show the world the things that matter to you the most. There are many different options for what to choose, but you may want to pick something deeply symbolic and meaningful. A meaningful tattoo is very individual and should have significance for the wearer. This could be anything from a motivational quote or the name of a loved one. Or a reminder of a painful memory and how far you have come since then or a positive experience. The piece should empower you and make you feel determined and strong.

55. Disney Tattoos

If you are a big fan of Disney, then you may be inspired to get one of your favorite scenes or characters inked onto your skin forever. Disney movies played an important part in their childhood for many people, and they remember them fondly. This could also be a great way to share a happy memory from when you were little or an excellent idea to get a matching piece with your sibling. Plus, there are so many different movies to be inspired by, and even a quote or a silhouette piece would be a great choice.

56. Star Tattoos

Star tattoos are some of the most popular pieces to get inked. The shape is so simple that it can be tattooed anywhere and in various sizes, from small to large, and more detailed. Stars are rich in meaning and are often symbolic of honor, destiny, guidance, hope, and direction. When you look into the night sky, it can bring you comfort or let your mind wander to the beauty of the world. They can also represent light during a time of darkness. The fantastic thing about getting a star tattoo is that there are many variations, each with slightly different symbolism. This allows you to tailor your inking to your preference. For example, a star and moon design or a shooting star.

57. Owl Tattoos

The owl is a majestic creature, often associated with wisdom and intelligence and mystery and witchcraft. In Native American cultures, the owl is also linked with the spirit world and can be seen as the guardian of knowledge. Not only is it visually appealing to get inked with this bird, but it can also have a variety of meanings and lends itself well to various designs. There are several species of owl to choose from, from the white snowy owl to the more common but no less beautiful barn owl. You can opt for a realistic portrayal of the animal or something cute and straightforward. The owl tattoo design is bound to turn heads.

58. Eagle Tattoos

Birds make fantastic choices for body art because there are so many to choose from, but, by far, one of the most beautiful and symbolic is the eagle. This mighty bird of prey is associated with wisdom, power, courage, and spirituality. It can also represent freedom, as it can fly away, and many watch them with awe as they soar across the sky. They also have particular importance in Native American culture, and their feathers are prized and used in rituals and ceremonies. If you are from the United States, an eagle tattoo may be connected to patriotism, as the bald eagle is the country's national animal.

59. Name Tattoos

What is not to love about a name tattoo? The idea is so simple yet so meaningful. Getting inked with a name can make for a very powerful inking, as it could be the name of a loved one, a way to honor someone who has passed, or to celebrate the birth of a child. There is so much meaning in a name. The simplicity also means that these tattoos can be inked anywhere, including the finger or behind the ear. You can also experiment with various fonts or even get inked in the handwriting of someone dear to you. That said, before getting someone's name, you should think about your relationship with them and whether it would be a good idea. For example, if it is a new romance, this may be a decision you wish to hold off on.

59. Tree Tattoos

Tree tattoos are a popular choice for women because of their versatility and symbolism. There are many different types of trees to choose from, each with slightly different meanings, but, in general, trees are associated with growth, strength, knowledge, wisdom, and renewal. They can also make a statement about the bonds we have with others, and the branches can represent different family members. Or the roots can indicate the strong foundation you share. Choosing to include the names of loved ones can be a nice touch and make your design more personal.

60. Gemini Tattoos

If your astrological sign is Gemini, then you may wish to honor this with a Gemini tattoo. Those born during the period May 21 and June 21 are considered Gemini, and the constellation of the Zodiac is made up of two twins, Castor and Pollux. Gemini is often associated with duality and how someone can exist and be two things at once. You can get Gemini twins inked or opt for a more subtle approach like the yin yang symbol. Others may be inspired by it being an Air element and find a creative way to incorporate that into their artwork.

61. White Tattoos

Most tattoos are created using standard black ink or, for those who want something brighter and bolder, with colored ink. Those are not the only options, though, and some women are drawn to white tattoos because they are subtle and unique. They are much less noticeable than black inkings and are therefore not as difficult to hide. Your design can also look delicate and pretty when created in white ink. There are a few downsides, though, including that white body art will fade much faster. They can also be more painful because the design has to be traced several times before the ink appears.

62. Cloud Tattoos

What could be more dreamy than a cloud tattoo? The fantastic thing about cloud designs is that they can be simple or detailed, allowing you to get them done in various sizes, and they can be tattooed anywhere. Clouds can have a positive or negative association; for some, they represent bad luck and are seen as an omen that something unfortunate will happen. While for others, clouds are connected to transformation, heaven, inspiration, and dreams. You can add to your cloud to change the meaning slightly and make for a more visually interesting piece. Options include rainbows, stars, and little cherubs.

63. Taurus Tattoos

A Taurus tattoo is a fantastic choice for those born from April 20 to May 20. The Zodiac is associated with the bull symbol and is an earth element, and some women may want to get inked with a design that incorporates these things. Another option would be to ink the constellation or look for a more abstract piece, representing the qualities and traits commonly associated with Taureres. These can include stubbornness, being set in their ways, loyalty, and dependability.

64. Memorial Tattoos

Before getting any tattoo, you should think about the reasons for getting it and whether you will regret it in the years to come. Some people make their decisions on a whim or end up with a romantic partner's name, only to break up weeks after. A meaningful choice that will stay relevant is a memorial tattoo. This piece is designed to honor a loved one you have lost and remind you how they impacted your life. There are many options, allowing you to create something unique and personal. Some may wish to keep it simple with the name, birth dates, and day of passing. Others may opt for a portrait piece, an angel, or even a favorite quote or cartoon character.

65. Christian Tattoos

If you feel a deep connection with your faith, you may want to honor it by incorporating it into your body art. Christian tattoos are popular choices for men and women who believe in the teachings of Christianity. Many symbols hold importance, including a cross, angels, praying hands, and the likeness of humanity's savior, Jesus Christ. There is no right or wrong decision, and it should be a way to express yourself. Some women may also prefer to keep it simple, choosing their favorite line from a Bible verse or a word or phrase that moves them.

66. Praying Hand Tattoos

A popular choice for religious individuals would be to get praying hands to tattoo. This symbol indicates the wearer's devotion to their faith and its importance in their life. The hands together show that they believe in God and the power that he holds, and this piece could also be connected to guidance, protection, and direction. Many people who opt for such a meaningful piece choose to ink it somewhere visible to them; for example, on the arm or the wrist. Getting it done in a location that you can look at every day can serve as a reminder of why you chose this design and bring you comfort or solace.

67. Octopus Tattoos

Octopus tattoos are popular nautical inkings that are rich in symbolism but are also visually interesting. The octopus is associated with mystery and intelligence but can represent fear and evil. For sailors, there is the legend of the Kraken, a gigantic sea monster that attacked ships. Deciding to get inked with this creature could instill fear or cause intimidation in others. Or show that you are not afraid. Some women may want to show their octopus wrapped around a vessel, pulling it into the depths of the sea, while others may opt for something pretty and colorful, showing the beauty of these creatures. There are so many interpretations and different designs that no two are quite alike.

68. Roman Numerals Tattoos

A roman numerals tattoo is a simple yet effective way to show the importance of a special date in your life. This could be anything from the date of your wedding, when your child was born, or even your birthday. It could also be used as a memorial piece, honoring a loved one who has passed. Since we do not use this numeric system daily, it is more interesting and unique, and people may have to spend a few moments working out the date. It is an incredibly personal tattoo and can be inked anywhere on the body and in various sizes. You may also wish to add to it with images such as roses, clocks, or skulls, each of which will give your design more meaning.

69. Mountain Tattoos

If you are a lover of nature and the outdoors or long to travel to new places and conquer new things, then the perfect inking for you is a mountain tattoo. In general, a mountain is associated with strength, constancy, and resilience. It can be tattooed by someone who has overcome a difficult time in their life as a reminder that there is beauty to be found or achievement after an uphill journey. You can also choose to get inked with the silhouette of your favorite mountain range, making your choice even more personal.

70. Aries Tattoos

The Aries zodiac is the perfect choice for someone drawn to the qualities that the sign represents. These include strength, energy, adventure, and courage. Those that are considered Aries are born between March 21 and April 20. The symbol is the ram, and it is a fire element, and as such, there are many ways to design it to make your piece interesting and personal. There are also various sizes, and your tattoo can be simple or detailed and include many different images. Choosing a zodiac tattoo is also a great way to feel connected to your birth date. Some also think that it brings luck and positivity into their daily lives.

71. Bee Tattoos

Your body art is a wonderful way to express yourself and share with the world the things that mean the most to you or the qualities you admire. A bee tattoo is a fantastic ink choice for women who want a piece that represents hard work, dedication, loyalty, and teamwork. The insect can express your desire to achieve great things in life or how you will not stop until you reach your goal. It can also symbolize your love for your family and how you would do anything for them. In addition, there are many ways to design your inking, including adding flowers, butterflies, or even birds. You could keep it simple with a line art honey bee or get creative with geometric-inspired artwork; the choice is yours.

72. Infinity Tattoos

The infinity tattoo symbol represents a never-ending cycle and has inspired many women. For some, this can mean an everlasting bond between them and someone special or expressing love with a romantic partner. If you feel very strongly about someone in your life, this could be an excellent way to convey that message. Some couples also opt for matching infinity pieces, including the names of a loved one and the date they started dating or got married. If you are a mathematics whizz, then this is an even more meaningful choice.

73. Tree of Life Tattoos

There are few symbols as powerful as the tree of life. It is associated with knowledge, wisdom, strength, and immortality and has importance in several cultures, including Norse and Celtic. It has been seen as the link between the spiritual and human world. In addition to the rich symbolism, a tree of life tattoo is often very detailed and beautiful. There are various ways to get it done, including in color or keeping it simple with black ink. The shape commonly features a large tree, with its branches spreading outwards and its roots intertwined in a circle. Some women may choose to add the names of their loved ones to each branch of the tree. Or to make the number of branches significant; for example, each branch corresponds to a family member.

74. Cherry Blossom Tattoos

The cherry blossom is a symbol of love, beauty, and impermanence. It could also be associated with Japanese pride, as it is the country's national flower. When the cherry blossom blooms, they are stunning, but they are not in season for long. For many, this is a metaphor for life or love and how short it can be, which is why we need to appreciate and celebrate each day. In addition to the meaning of this plant, it also makes for a stunning tattoo, especially when inked in color. There are many cherry blossom tattoos to choose from and various ways to design your piece. You could opt for a realistic portrayal or recreate it in a Japanese tattoo technique known for being bold and bright.

75. Cool Tattoos

What makes a cool tattoo is entirely up to you. It could be anything, from unique designs that make people do a double-take to badass tattoos that intimidate and make the wearer look tough. The location of your piece can also add to its cool factor, and some areas like the face or neck are rebellious choices, whereas others, like the hip or underboob, can be sexy and intimate. Get creative with your piece and pick something you will love looking at every day.

76. Cat Tattoos

If you are a cat lover, what better way to show the world this than with a cat tattoo? You could even get ink of your pet or favorite cat breed to make your piece more personal. Even if you don't own a pet cat, the appeal f getting feline-inspired body art remains because the animal is associated with luck, mystery, intelligence, and grace. For some, cats can also be an omen of bad luck, trickery, and even death. The way you choose to design your piece will help convey the meaning you associate with it. For example, potions, skulls, and snakes combined with your cat will add an element of mystery or give it a witchcraft feel.

78. Aquarius Tattoos

Those born between Jan. 20 and Feb. 18 are Aquarius. Aquarius is the water bearer and makes for a powerful and interesting piece, often associated with freedom and humanitarian causes. This makes it a thoughtful design for a woman who appreciates these qualities or wants to celebrate her birth date. There are several ways to get inked, including the constellation or a beautiful maiden holding a vase. Some people opt for a more abstract interpretation, such as a mermaid's tail.

79. Mandala Tattoos

Mandala tattoos are made up of a series of shapes and symbols that create a circular pattern. They are mesmerizing to look at and can be associated with tranquility, harmony, and balance. Women looking for a piece that can evoke a sense of calm when they look at it or remind themselves of the importance of finding harmony in their lives are often drawn to this design. Your mandala can be large and intricate, covering your thigh or upper arm, or can be kept small and inked on the wrist or the lower arm; places you can look at it every day.

80. Celtic Tattoos

If you have Celtic heritage or are interested in the Celts, then you may be drawn to the idea of a Celtic tattoo. They used these symbols for protection, to ward off evil and their enemies, and communicate. There are many symbols and animals, and trees that were deeply symbolic to the Celts. These include the Celtic Tree of Life, the Celtic Cross, The Irish Harp, and several knotted designs. The latter is one of the most common inspirations for body art. Their most simplistic interpretation represents the bond between humanity and nature, or family, eternal life and death, and everlasting love. A few knots to consider include the Triquetra or Trinity Knot and the Dara Knot.

81. Music Tattoos

If you are someone who is inspired by music, then why not get a music tattoo? All of us experience music in some way; we hear it on the radio, sing in the shower, and play an instrument. Music can provide an escape from the world, be comforting, and be beautiful and motivational. There are many options for your inking, including your favorite instrument or musical notes. Or quotes from a song you love. You could also get a design inspired by the past, such as a record player or a cassette. This could be because you love the music of decades past or as a way to honor previous generations, like your grandparents.

82. King and Queen Tattoos

A king and queen tattoo can make a statement about strength in relationships. These monarchs are more powerful together and often need each other to succeed and produce heirs. It has become a popular choice for couples to get inked to honor their romance. It can also signify that you want to stay by your partner's side forever. Or it could be a reminder that you can accomplish great things in life and strive to be the best version of yourself that you can be. There are many different options, including just inking the crowns of the king or queen or choosing playing cards.

83. Hummingbird Tattoo

A hummingbird tattoo is a stunning piece but also a symbolic one. The tiny creature is associated with good luck, beauty, hard work, and strength. In the ancient Aztec civilization, they believed that fallen warriors were reincarnated as hummingbirds, and thus, these birds can also be seen as a symbol of life, death, and rebirth. There are many different techniques and styles to choose from. Some women prefer the more simplistic and minimalistic approach, opting for line art or black ink, whereas others love bright and bold designs. Watercolor tattoos and American traditional styles are excellent options if you want your piece to get noticed.

84. Jesus Tattoos

Jesus Christ symbolizes sacrifice, unconditional love, and the divine. Those whose faith plays an important role in their life will be drawn to a Jesus tattoo to celebrate their devotion. Your piece can be of many things, combining several religious images, including the cross and praying hands, or focusing on a more specific design like Jesus and Mary. Each design is open to interpretation and personalized to reflect the wearer's thoughts and feelings. This can also be done by adding quotes or Bible verses.

85. Joker Tattoo

There are few designs as striking as a Joker tattoo. The supervillain makes for an interesting and symbolic inking, associated with rebellion, evil, madness, and our potential to become unhinged. There are also many different interpretations of what the Joker looks like, from the original DC Comic designs to his appearance in various films, allowing versatility with how you portray him. You can also combine the Joker with other images to alter the meaning; this can include Harley Quinn or his iconic laugh; HAHAHA.

86. Tiger Tattoo

A tiger tattoo is a wonderful choice for someone who wants to make a statement with their body art. The big cat represents strength and power and has great importance in several cultures. It is a powerful predator at the top of the food chain and is respected and feared. They are often featured in Chinese and Japanese folklore and look great when inked in these tattoo styles. Or you could opt for a realistic approach, opting for a highly detailed image. In addition, you could ink a tiger cub, which represents innocence and is a wonderful way to celebrate your children, or could be a nod to the simpler times of your childhood.

87. Neo Traditional Tattoo

Neo Traditional tattoos are defined by their bold outlines, clean lines, and bright color palette. They share many similarities with American Traditional tattoo styles but are more detailed and have a greater depth of dimension. You are also less restricted with the imagery you choose, and Neo Traditional designs can be of almost anything, from portrait pieces to nature-inspired artwork. This is ideal for anyone who wants a style that will demand attention because the technique is eye-catching and feels a little rebellious. Get inked somewhere visible to show off your tattoo, or keep it hidden on the back or upper thigh; the choice is yours!

88. Mushroom Tattoo

Mushrooms have inspired many tattoos because they can be created to look simple or detailed. There are many styles to choose from, letting you experiment with outlines and colors and opting to create a realistic tattoo or a cartoonish one, like the iconic red mushroom from the Super Mario games. Mushrooms are symbolic, too, often associated with life and energy. This will make sense to you if you are an avid gamer, as mushrooms are often used as a power-up tool. Your design can also have a deeper meaning associated with it, representing the positive things in your life and inspiring you. It could be related to friends and family.

89. Trash Polka

One of the boldest and most eye-catching techniques for body art is the Trash Polka tattoo. It is a brilliant blend of abstract and realistic designs, done predominantly in a mix of red and black ink. The style was created by tattoo artists Simone Pfaff and Volker Merschky from Germany and has become popular because the designs are so expressive. The finished product feels chaotic and rebellious. The subject matter can combine several things, letting you tailor the designs to your preference.

90. Temporary Tattoo

If you love the idea of body art but are not ready to commit to it forever, why not try a temporary tattoo? The appeal of temporary tattoos is that they let you experiment with different designs, giving you a better idea of where you may want the real thing. You can try out multiple placements before getting inked, and you can experiment with different sizes. If you are unsure whether a tattoo would look good on you, this is also a way to figure that out without investing any time, money, or discomfort. Or perhaps you do not want to get a real tattoo at all, in which case temporary designs are a nice alternative and can still be expressive and fun.

91. Anime Tattoo

Anime refers to the Japanese style of animation. It is popular worldwide, and there are many different characters to choose from, with detailed storylines that can be moving and inspiring. If you want an anime tattoo that represents your likes and reflects something that you are passionate about, this is a great choice. You can keep your design simple, focusing on the logos from your favorite anime, or you can get tattooed with a character. You may also wish to combine several images to tell a story, which can be done with a sleeve tattoo.

92. Grim Reaper Tattoo

The grim reaper is an intimidating image for a tattoo and can seem morbid. But it also makes a powerful statement about life and death. Life is uncertain, and the only certain thing is that we do not live forever. This can be terrifying and empowering at the same time. Your grim reaper or angel of death design can be a way to remind yourself to live each moment to its fullest. It can be about the importance of embracing life and doing everything you want to do while you have the chance. Or it could be a warning to others that you are someone who is not afraid and should not be messed with. There are many interpretations of the grim reaper tattoo, letting you personalize your piece to reflect your thoughts and feelings.

93. Naruto Tattoos

One of the most popular and well-known anime characters is Naruto Uzumaki, from the manga Naruto series. It is not hard to see why this series would inspire people. In addition to the artwork consisting of beautiful, colorful, and detailed imagery, it is also a symbolic choice. You do not have to ink Naruto Uzumaki, but it can be any of the characters or images that reference Naruto; this option will appeal to dedicated fans and may not be immediately recognizable to the general public.

94. Egyptian Tattoos

Egyptian tattoos are an excellent design for someone fascinated by the culture or have a deep respect for its history. It can be a way to honor your heritage, or it could be because you are drawn to the symbolism associated with the symbols of Ancient Egypt. And there are many to choose from, from Anubis, the Ba Ba, the Ankh, and the Eye of Horus. You can also include multiple images to create a sleeve tattoo, telling a story and reflecting your thoughts and feelings. Each piece is rich in history and makes a thought-provoking choice for a tattoo. Show it off by opting to get inked on the arm, wrist, or hand. Or cover up your design on the back or upper thigh.

95. Harry Potter Tattoos

Harry Potter continues to be as relevant today as it was decades earlier when the first book was released in 1997. It is hard to believe that J. K. Rowling's creation is as old as it is, as it continues to inspire countless fans. Perhaps you want to get inked with a Harry Potter design to honor the good memories from your childhood? Or maybe you want to share your thoughts and feelings by getting inked with your favorite characters or symbols that are meaningful to you. Lovers of the wizarding world have many things to choose from, allowing them to adapt their tattoo to suit their preferences. This could be anything from detailed images of Harry Potter, Ron Weasley, and Hermione Granger to simple designs of the lightning bolt scar or Harry's glasses.

96. Palm Tree Tattoo

The palm tree is a popular choice of tattoo for those who want something that represents life and relaxation. It can also mean summer, vacations, and relaxation and could be a great way to remind yourself to take a break or the importance of travel and escaping the daily grind. A palm tree could also be a cute way to honor your favorite holiday, serving as a memory of your time with your loved ones or on your own. The palm tree can also have a religious association, symbolizing Jesus' entry into Jerusalem. This can be a design to celebrate your faith.

97. Patchwork Tattoo

When choosing a tattoo, many people opt for the same style and follow a specific theme, especially if the artwork is big, like a leg sleeve or a sleeve tattoo. These pieces are detailed and carefully placed together to look cohesive. However, patchwork tattoos do not need to be seamlessly joined together, and the space between the different images makes them each stand out. This is an appealing choice if you want to combine multiple themes. In some ways, patchwork designs give you more freedom with placement and are versatile as you can easily combine several different images. It is still a good idea to stick to the same color scheme and style for the best results.

98. Flash Tattoo

A tattoo flash or flash tattoo is a premade design that you will find in your chosen tattoo studio. They often appear in a book or are decorated on the walls, giving you a better idea of what the artist can do and the different designs and styles. These pieces are not custom-made; they are often cheaper and less time-consuming to create. This can be an appealing choice for someone undecided on the design they want. You can also combine several flash tattoos.

99. Anchor Tattoo

The anchor tattoo symbolizes strength, endurance, stability, and calmness. It keeps vessels in place while at sea, preventing them from drifting in the current. It is rich in symbolism, making for a powerful tattoo design. If you are a sailor or spend a lot of time at sea, this is an obvious choice. But even for those who have never ventured at sea, this is an appealing design because it can represent the hard times in your life and remind you that you are strong and can weather any storm. Your tattoo can be as simple or detailed as you wish, and you can combine other nautical imagery depending on how big you want your design to be.

100. Quote Tattoo

A quote tattoo is an excellent design choice for your next piece. Quotes can motivate and encourage. They can make you laugh and bring a smile to your face, and you can draw inspiration from anywhere. It could be from your favorite book, a childhood film that you love, or something someone has said to you. You can get a quote tattooed to honor a special bond you have with a loved one, including a parent or a best friend. Or celebrate the love of your life. The placement for your inking is just as important, and popular locations include the spine, chest, and thigh.

Chapter 7

Tattoo risks and side effects.

Most of the risks and side effects from tattoos occur when the tattoo is still fresh. At this point, your skin is still healing, so proper aftercare is necessary to prevent complications.

- Skin infection

While tattooing is an art, the actual process is technically one that causes injury to your skin. This includes both the upper (epidermal) and middle (dermal) layers of skin.

Your skin needs to recover after you get new ink, so your tattoo artist will give you tips on how to prevent infection.

An infection can also occur if nonsterile water is mixed with the ink before injection.

You're most vulnerable to a skin infection from a tattoo within the first two weeks. Symptoms include redness, itchiness, and discharge. The area may also become swollen.

If the infection spreads, you can have other symptoms, such as a fever. In severe cases, infections can be chronic (ongoing).

- Allergic reactions

Some people might develop an allergic reaction after getting a tattoo. This is usually related to the ink — especially if it contains plastic — and not the needling process itself. Red, yellow, blue, and green pigments tend to be the most allergenic.

Symptoms of an allergic reaction from tattoos can include a red rash, hives, and severe itchiness. Swelling can occur too. These effects can occur years after you get the tattoo.

- Keloid scarring

Tattoos have the potential to scar. This is especially true if your tattoo doesn't heal properly, or if you have an infection or allergic reaction. Eventually, you can also develop keloid scars — these consist of raised bumps that contain old scar tissue.

- Complications with MRIs

If your doctor orders an MRI scan, there's a slight chance that the test could interact with your tattoo. Some of the side effects include swelling and itchiness afterward, but they tend to go away on their own.

Your risk of such reactions could be higher if your tattoo was inked with low-quality pigments or if the tattoo is old.

Talk to a doctor if you're concerned about your tattoo interfering with an MRI scan. According to the Mayo Clinic, this reaction is relatively rare.

- Sterilization of needles

A reputable tattoo artist will use sterilized needles. Many states require sterilized needles by law although this can vary by state.

Not using sterilized needles increases your risk of infection and can also pose the risk of transmitting blood-borne illnesses, including HIV, hepatitis C, and methicillin-resistant Staphylococcus aureus (MRSA).

- Can hide skin cancer

Another risk of getting a tattoo is that it can hide possible signs of skin cancer or another skin condition. These include the telling moles, red patches, and other signs that might be associated with a skin issue that could go undetected.

- Is tattoo ink safe?

Tattoo ink is much safer than it used to be. However, there's a possibility that you can be sensitive to certain colors, especially brighter pigments.

The U.S. Food and Drug Administration (FDA) has strict standards about labeling inks to prevent cross-contamination, but you could still be vulnerable if such practices aren't followed. Ask your provider whether the ink is completely sterile to reduce your risk.

Another issue relates to the components of the tattoo pigments. Traces of nickel, lead, and other cancer-causing agents in 65 tattoo inks.

Also, some inks contain the same chemicals used in car paint and printer ink, but the agency doesn't regulate these materials.

More tests involving the safety of tattoo inks are needed to determine the overall risks for people wanting to get tattoos.

- Precautions

One of the best ways you can decrease the risks of getting a tattoo is to do a little homework first. You have to be 18 or older to get a tattoo in the United States., so shops or individual artists who do ink on anyone younger should raise a red flag.

Once you've decided that you want to get a tattoo, find the right provider. Word-of-mouth is a good place to start. You can also check out the shop ahead of time to see the artists' licenses, experience, and what types of ink they use.

- Takeaway

Despite the improved safety of tattoos, it's important to work with an experienced tattoo artist at a reputable shop to reduce your risk of side effects. Proper aftercare on your part is also important to reduce scarring and other risks.

While tattoos aren't completely risk-free, knowing the potential effects ahead of time can reduce your chances of side effects. Talk to your tattoo artist about any concerns you may have.

www.ingramcontent.com/pod-product-compliance
Lightning Source LLC
Chambersburg PA
CBHW060439220526
45465CB00008B/3202